YOUR PRAYERS
AND MINE

Compiled by

ELIZABETH YATES

Decorations by

NORA S. UNWIN

HOUGHTON MIFFLIN COMPANY BOSTON

The Riverside Press Cambridge

Grateful acknowledgment is made to the following:

The Devin-Adair Company, New York, for permission to use the prayers BE THOU MY VISION and HOSPITALITY PRAYER from their book 1000 YEARS OF IRISH POETRY edited by Kathleen Hoagland.

Harper and Brothers, New York, for permission to use the FORMOSAN PRAYER and JAPANESE PRAYER from their book THE WORLD AT ONE IN PRAYER by Dr. Frederick S. Fleming.

Gresham's, Texas, for permission to use the prayer on page 54 from their book THE OLDEST CHRISTIAN HYMN BOOK A.D. 100 by Reverend Michael Mar-Yosip.

E. P. Dutton and Company, Inc., New York, and John Murray, London, for permission to use five prayers, three by L. H. M. Soulsby, one by Sir Clement Bailache, and one by J. H. Jowett from their book A CHAIN OF PRAYER ACROSS THE AGES by Selina Fitzherbert Fox.

Longmans Green and Company, Limited, London, for permission to use three prayers from their book SHORT PRAYERS by L. H. M. Soulsby.

For
Our Mothers
who taught us
to pray

Elizabeth

Nora

CONTENTS

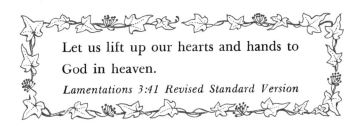

Let us lift up our hearts and hands to God in heaven.

Lamentations 3:41 Revised Standard Version

PRAYER is talking with God and listening to God. It is a secret conversation between friends. The words may be no more than a cry for help in the dark night of pain or sorrow, a shout of joy in the bright morning of work, a plea for strength in the noontime of continuing tasks, a quiet return of thanks in the evening of rest and acccomplishment. Whatever they may be, they are not so important as the stillness which follows them. Prayer is a pursuit in which everyone participates. No matter what outward differences divide us, we are all one in the eyes of the Father; we are all equally beloved and we receive equally of His care. To pray is not so much to bend the knee as it is to fold the hands in quietness and uplift the heart in readiness.

Any form of prayer is like the key that opens a door. A small key it may be, taken from an inner pocket, a key grown smooth from much handling. Responding to its turning, the door opens slowly — into what stillness, down what avenues of radiance, only the one who prays knows; but the experience, no matter how long or short, is not unmarked in our lives. "He who rises from prayer a better man," George Meredith wrote, "his prayer is answered."

Here, in this book, are prayers gathered from many sources and many nations, prayers that have been used through many centuries of time; yet their approach is the same. It is direct and simple and intimate. A rim of holiness bounds the day that begins and ends with prayer, the day that finds us keeping often our tryst with God. To pause mentally, where we are and in the midst of what we are doing, and there to be aware of God's presence, enables us to continue in what we are doing as though we were always in His presence.

"Oh, do not pray for easy lives," Phillips Brooks said once. "Do not pray for tasks equal to your powers. Pray for powers equal to your tasks. Then the doing of your work will be no miracle; but you will be the miracle. And every day you will wonder at yourself, at the richness of life which has come to you by the grace of God."

It is through prayer that we learn to walk confidently with God, to face life courageously, and to act lovingly with our fellows; for prayer is the mountaintop of vision from which we see the good that can be ours.

ELIZABETH YATES

O Lord, in the morning Thou dost hear my voice;
In the morning I prepare a sacrifice for Thee,
and watch.

Psalm 5:3   Revised Standard Version

WE GIVE THEE HEARTY thanks for the rest of the past night and for the gift of a new day, with its opportunities of pleasing Thee. Grant that we may so pass its hours in the perfect freedom of Thy service that at eventide we may again give thanks unto Thee.

Daybreak Office of the Eastern Church
Third Century

LORD, as Thy mercies do surround us, so grant that our returns of duty may abound; and let this day manifest our gratitude by doing something well-pleasing to Thee.

Edward Lake, England
Seventeenth Century

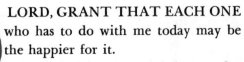 **LORD, GRANT THAT EACH ONE** who has to do with me today may be the happier for it.

Let it be given me each hour today what I shall say, and grant me the wisdom of a loving heart that I may say the right thing rightly.

Help me to enter into the mind of everyone who talks with me, and keep me alive to the feelings of each one present.

Give me a quick eye for little kindnesses, that I may be ready in doing them and gracious in receiving them.

Give me quick perception of the feelings and needs of others, and make me eager-hearted in helping them.

Lucy H. M. Soulsby, England
Twentieth Century

LET US TAKE hands and help, this day we are alive together, look up on high and thank the God of all.
On a bench in Kew Gardens, England

HEAVENLY FATHER, WHO HAST filled the world with beauty, open, we beseech Thee, our eyes to behold Thy gracious hand in all Thy works; that rejoicing in Thy whole creation, we may learn to serve Thee with gladness.

Book of Common Prayer
Sixteenth Century

O LORD, grant that I may do Thy will as if it were my will,
That Thou mayest do my will as if it were Thy will.

Rabbi Gamaliel
First Century

ALMIGHTY and everlasting God, grant that our wills be ever meekly subject to Thy will, and our hearts be ever honestly ready to serve Thee.

Roman Breviary

MAY THE STRENGTH OF GOD pilot me, the power of God preserve me today.

May the wisdom of God instruct me, the eye of God watch over me, the ear of God hear me, the word of God give me sweet talk, the hand of God defend me, the way of God guide me.

Christ be with me. Christ before me.

Christ after me. Christ in me.

Christ under me. Christ over me.

Christ on my right hand. Christ on my left hand.

Christ on this side. Christ on that side.

Christ at my back.

Christ in the head of everyone to whom I speak.

Christ in the mouth of every person who speaks to me.

Christ in the eye of every person who looks upon me.

Christ in the ear of every person who hears me today.

St. Patrick, Ireland
Fifth Century

LORD, LET US learn from the experiences of today the lessons which Thou meanest today to teach.

Sir Clement Bailhache, England
Twentieth Century

HE who directs the sparrow's tender flight,
And sees him safely reach the heartless ground,
Guide thee in all thy passages aright,
And grant thy course be sure, thy resting sound.

Richard Zouche, England
Seventeenth Century

MY LORD, I am ready on the threshold of this new day to go forth armed with Thy power, seeking adventure on the high road, to right wrong, to overcome evil, to serve Thee bravely, faithfully, joyously.

On a Knight's Tomb
Church Icomb, England
Thirteenth Century

BLESS ALL who worship Thee, from the rising of the sun unto the going down of the same.

Of Thy goodness, give us;
With Thy love, inspire us;
By Thy spirit, guide us;
By Thy power, protect us;
In Thy mercy, receive us now and always.

Ancient Collect

LORD, MAKE ME AN INSTRUMENT of Thy peace; where there is hatred, let me sow love; where there is injury, pardon; where there is doubt, faith; where there is despair, hope; where there is darkness, light; where there is sadness, joy.

O Divine Master, grant that I may not so much seek to be consoled as to console; to be understood as to understand; to be loved as to love. For it is in giving that we receive, it is in pardoning that we are pardoned, and it is in dying that we are born to eternal life.

St. Francis of Assisi, Italy
Thirteenth Century

WHAT IS BEFORE US we know not, but this we know: that all things are ordered and sure. Everything is ordered with unerring wisdom and unbounded love by Thee, our God, who art Love. Grant us in all things to see Thy hand.

C. Simeon, England
Eighteenth Century

THINE is the day, O Lord, and Thine is the night,
Grant that the Sun of Righteousness may abide in our hearts
To drive away the darkness of evil thoughts.

Gelasian Sacramentary
Fifth Century

O FATHER, this day may bring some hard task to our life, or some hard trial to our love. We may grow weary, or sad, or hopeless in our lot. But, Father, our whole life until now has been one great proof of Thy care. Bread has come for our bodies, thoughts to our minds, love to our hearts, and all from Thee. So help us, we implore Thee, while we stand still on this side of all that the day may bring, to resolve that we will trust Thee this day to shine into any gloom of the mind, to stand by us in any trial of our love, and to give us rest in Thy good time as we need.

May this day be full of a power that shall bring us near to Thee, and make us more like Thee; and, O God, may we so trust Thee this day, that when the day is done our trust shall be firmer than ever.

Robert Collyer, Wales
Nineteenth Century

TAKE, LORD, AND RECEIVE MY entire liberty, my memory and my understanding, my imagination and my whole will.

All that I am and all that I have, Thou hast given me and I surrender it all to Thee now that Thou mayest dispose of it according to Thy will.

Give me but Thy love and Thy grace and I am rich enough and have nothing more to desire.

St. Ignatius Loyola, Spain
Sixteenth Century

TEACH US, good Lord, to serve Thee as Thou deservest:

To give and not to count the cost;
To fight and not to heed the wounds;
To strive and not to seek for rest;
To labor and not to ask for reward,
Saving the knowledge that we do Thy will.

St. Ignatius Loyola, Spain
Sixteenth Century

AKE FROM US, O GOD, ALL PRIDE and vanity, all boasting and frowardness, and give us the true courage that shows itself by gentleness; the true wisdom that shows itself by simplicity; and the true power that shows itself by modesty.

Guide us, teach us, and strengthen, O Lord, we beseech Thee, until we become as Thou wouldst have us be: pure, gentle, truthful, high-minded, courteous, generous, able, dutiful and useful, for Thy honor and glory.

Charles Kingsley, England
Nineteenth Century

OUR FATHER, may the world not mould us today, but may we be so strong as to help to mould the world.

J. H. Jowett, England
Nineteenth Century

O LORD, Thou knowest how busy I must be this day; if I forget Thee, do not Thou forget me.

Sir Jacob Astley, England
Seventeenth Century

LORD, my God, how surely Thou dost
come through my window
With the morning sun.
I arise from my bed to find Thee.
Thou sittest at my table;
I show Thee my thoughts.
Thou choosest from amongst them what I am to do;
Thou appointest me to my task.
Thou pourest strength into me.
Before Thee do I sit down and work.
When I am empty Thou fillest me.
When I am descended into the midst of the trivialities
    of earth
Thou givest me wings to fly up.
Thou suppliest me with all things.
Thou rewardest me with joy —
Yea, with great joy dost Thou reward me;
In the midst of my work I lift up my voice and sing;
Going and coming I dance.
And when Thou hast judged the length of my day
Thou stoppest the river of my thoughts from flowing,
And makest me to lie down upon my bed and sleep.

Anonymous, United States
Twentieth Century

ATHER, I know that all my life
Is portioned out for me;
The changes that are sure to come
    I do not fear to see:
But I ask Thee for a present mind
Intent on pleasing Thee.
I ask Thee for a thoughtful love
Through constant watching wise,
To meet the glad with joyful smiles
    And to wipe the weeping eyes;
And a heart at leisure from itself,
To soothe and sympathize.
Wherever in the world I am,
In whatso'er estate,
I have a fellowship of hearts
    To keep and cultivate:
And a work of lowly love to do
For the Lord on whom I wait.
So I ask Thee for the daily strength
To none that ask denied;
And a mind to blend with outward
        life
    While keeping at Thy side:
Content to fill a little space
If Thou be glorified.

Anna L. Waring, United States
Parting Hymn at Abbot Academy

11

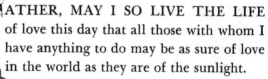

ATHER, MAY I SO LIVE THE LIFE of love this day that all those with whom I have anything to do may be as sure of love in the world as they are of the sunlight.

Anonymous, United States
Twentieth Century

GRANT US, O Lord, to pass this day in gladness and in peace, without stumbling and without strain; that, reaching the eventide victorious over all temptation, we may praise Thee, Eternal God, who art blessed and dost govern all things, world without end.

Mozarabic Liturgy, Spain
Sixth Century

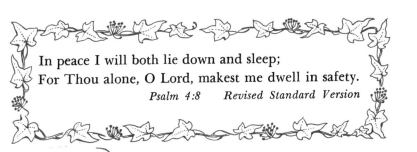

In peace I will both lie down and sleep;
For Thou alone, O Lord, makest me dwell in safety.

Psalm 4:8   Revised Standard Version

IF AT NIGHT when day is done
Kneeling by your bed,
You can only think of Him
Though no words are said;
If in crowds you think of Him
Who gives you light and air,
God will know in His love
That you mean a prayer.

Source Unknown

THE BLESSING of darkness lies over the world,
Not a leaf is stirring,
Not a bird is twittering;
Yet, here in the stillness,
I am as sure of Your presence,
   dear God,
As I am of my own heart beating.

Anonymous, United States
Twentieth Century

13

Gᴏᴅ be in my head, and in my understanding;
God be in my eyes, and in my looking;
God be in my mouth, and in my speaking;
God be in my heart, and in my thinking;
God be at my end, and in my departing.

Sarum Primer, England
Fifteenth Century

O Lᴏʀᴅ, we have a busy world around us. Eye, ear, and thought will be needed for all our work to be done in the world. Now ere we again enter upon it on the morrow we would commit eye, ear, and thought to Thee. Do Thou bless them and keep their work Thine, that as through Thy natural laws our hearts beat and our blood flows without any thought of ours for them, so our spiritual life may hold on its course at those times when our minds cannot consciously turn to Thee to commit each particular thought to Thy service.

Dr. Thomas Arnold
Used daily at Rugby School, England
Nineteenth Century

14

ORD, WE THANK THEE FOR THIS place in which we dwell; for the love that unites us; for the peace accorded us this day; for the hope with which we expect the morrow; for the health, the work, the food, and the bright skies that make our lives delightful; for our friends in all parts of the earth, and our friendly helpers.

Give us grace and strength to forbear and to persevere.

Give us courage and gaiety and the quiet mind.

Spare to us our friends, soften to us our enemies.

Bless us, if it may be, in all our innocent endeavors. If it may not, give us strength to encounter that which is to come, that we be brave in peril, constant in tribulation, temperate in wrath, and in all changes of fortune, and down to the gates of death, loyal and loving to one another.

Robert Louis Stevenson, Scotland
Nineteenth Century

LORD, WHEN WE sleep let us not be afraid, but let our sleep be sweet, that we may be enabled to serve Thee on the morrow.

William Laud, England
Seventeenth Century

B E THOU my vision, O Lord of my heart,
Naught is all else to me, save that Thou art.

Thou my best thought by day and by night,
Waking or sleeping, Thy presence my light.

Be Thou my wisdom, Thou my true word;
I ever with Thee, Thou with me, Lord.

Thou my great Father, I Thy dear son;
Thou in me dwelling, I with Thee one.

Be Thou my battle-shield, sword for the fight,
Be Thou my dignity, Thou my delight.

Thou my soul's shelter, Thou my high tower;
Raise Thou me heavenward, power of my power.

Riches I heed not, nor man's empty praise,
Thou mine inheritance now and always.

Thou, and Thou only, first in my heart,
High king of heaven, my treasure Thou art.

King of the seven heavens, grant me for dole,
Thy love in my heart, Thy light in my soul.

Thy light from my soul, Thy love from my heart,
King of the seven heavens, may they never depart.

With the high king of heaven, after victory won,
May I reach heaven's joys, O bright heaven's sun!

Heart of my own heart, whatever befall,
Still be my vision, O Ruler of all.

Anonymous, Ireland
Eighth Century
Translated by Eleanor Hull

LORD CHRIST, Thou gavest Thyself for me;
Behold here I am,
And here I give myself to Thee.

Jeremiah Dyke, England
Seventeenth Century

Lord, I give myself to Thee, I trust Thee wholly.

Thou art wiser than I, more loving to me than I myself.

Deign to fulfil Thy high purposes in me whatever they be.

Work in and through me.

I am born to serve Thee, to be Thine, to be Thy instrument.

I ask not to see, I ask not to know,

I ask simply to be used.

John Henry Newman, England
Nineteenth Century

Watch Thou, dear Lord, with those who wake, or watch, or weep tonight, and give Thine angels charge over those who sleep. Tend Thy sick ones, O Lord Christ. Rest Thy weary ones. Bless Thy dying ones. Soothe Thy suffering ones. Pity Thine afflicted ones. Shield Thy joyous ones. And all, for Thy love's sake.

St. Augustine, Africa
Fifth Century

From ghoulies and ghosties and long-leggity beasties, and all things that go bump in the night, Good Lord, deliver us.

Ancient Invocation

18

FATHER, BEFORE I CLOSE MY EYES, I would look back over the day to see if I have used it well.

Whatever came, did I turn it to good?

Whatever opportunity arose, did I see it as service to Thee?

If my answer is Yes, that is the praise of joyful lips; but if uncertainty clothes my mind, let it become readiness to greet the morrow and serve Thee better.

So during the night watches my meditation shall be sweet.

Anonymous, United States
Twentieth Century

To THE SUN that has shone all day,
To the moon that has gone away,
To the milk-white, silk-white, lily-white star,
A last good-night wherever you are.

James Guthrie, England
Twentieth Century

EVENING STAR, send for me.

Night prayer of the Osage
Indian Children
Midwestern United States

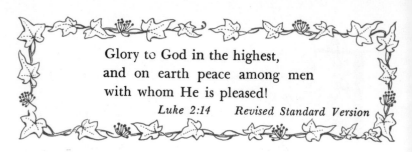

Glory to God in the highest,
and on earth peace among men
with whom He is pleased!

Luke 2:14   Revised Standard Version

HOLY Child of Bethlehem,
Descend to us, we pray;
Cast out our sin, and enter in,
Be born in us today.

*Phillips Brooks, United States
Nineteenth Century*

INTO THY presence we bear our gifts,
Each one a wise man of old:
    Incense the praise of grateful hearts,
    Prayer more precious than gold:
    Myrrh is the gift that costs us most
    For it is our sorrow and pain,
But we give it to Thee that Thy son
May turn it to gladness again.

*Anonymous, United States
Twentieth Century*

20

OVING looks the large-eyed cow,
Loving stares the long-eared ass
At Heaven's glory in the grass!
Child, with added human birth,
Come to bring the child of earth
Glad repentance, cheerful mirth,
And a seat beside the hearth
At the Father's knee —

Make us peaceful as the cow;
Make us patient as the ass;
Make us quiet as thou art now;
Make us strong as thou wilt be.
Make us always know and see
We are His as well as thou.

George MacDonald, Scotland
Nineteenth Century

O MOST merciful Redeemer, Friend and Brother,
May we know Thee more clearly,
Love Thee more dearly,
And follow Thee more nearly,
For Thine own sake.

St. Richard of Chichester, England
Thirteenth Century

KING of the elements, Love, Father of Bliss,
In my pilgrimage from airt to airt,
   From airt to airt,
May each evil be a good to me,
May each sorrow be a gladness to me,
And may Thy son be my foster-brother,
Oh, may Thy son be my foster-brother.

Holy Spirit, Spirit of Light,
A pilgrim I, throughout the night,
   Throughout the night.
Love my heart pure as the stars,
Love my heart pure as the stars,
Nor fear I then the spells of evil,
   The spells of evil.

Jesus, son of the virgin-pure,
Be thou my pilgrim-staff throughout the land.
   Throughout the land.
Thy love in all my thought,
Thy likeness in my face,
May I heart-warm to others and they heart-warm to
   me,
   For the love of Thee,
   For the love of Thee.

Ancient Gaelic Rune

22

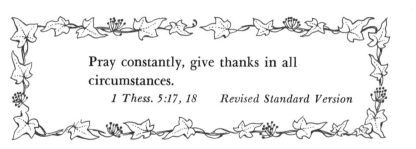

Pray constantly, give thanks in all circumstances.

1 Thess. 5:17, 18   Revised Standard Version

DEAR GOD, BE good to me. The sea is so wide and my boat is so small.

Prayer of the Breton Fishermen, France

GOD, IN WHOM and of whom are all things, grant me the vision to see all in Thee.

In doing Thy will is my time for accomplishing the work Thou hast given me to do.

In loving Thee are all those whom Thou hast given me to love.

No one or thing can stray from Thy presence. All that makes up my world is safe in Thee, for all is Thine.

Anonymous, United States Twentieth Century

 GOD, OF SURPASSING GOOD-
ness, whom the round world with one
voice doth praise for Thy sweet benig-
nity; we pray Thee to remove from us
all error, so we may perform Thy will.

Sarum Breviary, England
Eleventh Century

LORD, I KNOW NOT what I ought to ask of Thee;
Thou only knowest what I need; Thou lovest me
better than I know how to love myself. O Father,
give to Thy child that which he himself knows not
how to ask. I present myself before Thee, I open
my heart to Thee. Behold my needs which I know
not myself; see and do according to Thy tender
mercy. I offer myself in sacrifice. I yield myself to
Thee. I would have no other desire than to ac-
complish Thy will. Teach me to pray. Pray Thyself
in me.

François de la Mothe Fénelon, France
Seventeenth Century

24

 E BESEECH THEE, O LORD,
that Thou wouldst keep our
tongues from evil, and our lips
from speaking guile; that, as Thy
holy angels ever sing Thy praises
in heaven, so with our tongues may we at all times
glorify Thee on earth.

Roman Breviary

G IVE ME, O Lord, a steadfast heart, which no unworthy affection may drag downwards; give me an
unconquered heart, which no tribulation can wear
out; give me an upright heart, which no unworthy
purpose may tempt aside.

Bestow upon me also, O Lord my God, understanding to know Thee, diligence to seek Thee,
wisdom to find Thee, and a faithfulness that may
finally embrace Thee.

St. Thomas Aquinas, Italy
Thirteenth Century

O LORD, hear my prayer, fulfil my desire to my
good, and to the praise of Thy holy name.

Sarum Breviary, England
Eleventh Century

AY I BE NO MAN'S ENEMY, AND may I be the friend of that which is eternal and abides. May I never quarrel with those nearest me; and if I do, may I be reconciled quickly. May I never devise evil against any man; if any man devise evil against me, may I escape uninjured and without the need of hurting him. May I love, seek, and attain only that which is good. May I wish for all men's happiness and envy none. May I never rejoice in the ill-fortune of one who has wronged me. When I have done or said what is wrong, may I never wait for the rebuke of others, but always rebuke myself until I make amends.

May I win no victory that harms either me or my opponent.

May I reconcile friends who are wroth with one another. May I, to the extent of my power, give all needful help to my friends and to all who are in want. May I never fail a friend in danger. When visiting those in grief may I be able by gentle and healing words to soften their pain.

May I respect myself.

May I always keep tame that which rages within me.

May I accustom myself to be gentle, and never be angry with people because of circumstances. May I never discuss who is wicked and what wicked things he has done, but know good men and follow in their footsteps.

Eusebius, pre-Christian
probably Fourth Century B.C.

GIVE ME BEAUTY in the inward soul; and may the inward and the outer be at one. May I reckon wisdom to be wealth, and may I have so much gold as a temperate man and only he can bear and carry.

This prayer, I think, is enough for me.

Socrates, Greece
Fifth Century B.C.

ORD, purge our eyes to see
Within the seed a tree,
Within the glowing egg a bird,
Within the shroud a butterfly.

Till taught by such, we see
Beyond all creatures Thee,
And hearken to Thy tender word,
And hear it, "Fear not: it is I."

Christina Rossetti, England
Nineteenth Century

O LORD, grant us to love Thee;
Grant that we may love those that love Thee;
Grant that we may do the deeds that win Thy love.
Make the love of Thee to be dearer to us
Than ourselves and our families,
Than wealth, and even than cool water.

Mohammed, Arabia
Sixth Century

O GOD, of Thy goodness, give me Thyself, for only
in Thee have I all.

Lady Julian of Norwich, England
Fourteenth Century

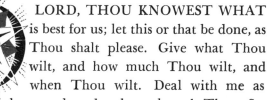 LORD, THOU KNOWEST WHAT is best for us; let this or that be done, as Thou shalt please. Give what Thou wilt, and how much Thou wilt, and when Thou wilt. Deal with me as Thou thinkest good, and as best pleaseth Thee. Set me where Thou wilt, and deal with me in all things just as Thou wilt.

Behold, I am Thy servant, prepared for all things; for I desire not to live unto myself, but unto Thee, and O, that I could do it worthily and perfectly!

Thomas à Kempis, Germany
Fifteenth Century

LORD, DO THOU turn me all into love, and all my love into obedience, and let my obedience be without interruption, and then I hope Thou wilt accept such a return as I can make. Make me to be something that Thou delightest in, and Thou shalt have all that I am or have from Thee, even whatsoever Thou makest fit for Thyself.

Jeremy Taylor, England
Seventeenth Century

LORD, WE PRAY NOT FOR TRAN-quillity, nor that our tribulations may cease; we pray for Thy spirit and Thy love, that Thou grant us strength and grace to overcome adversity.

Savonarola, Italy
Fifteenth Century

O CHRIST OUR LORD, who art the physician of salvation, grant unto all that are sick the aid of heavenly healing.

Mozarabic Liturgy, Spain
Sixth Century

GRANT UNTO Thy people, we beseech Thee, O Lord, health both of body and mind; that, persevering in good works, they may ever be defended by Thy mighty protection.

Gregorian Sacramentary
Eighth Century

GIVE ME a good digestion, Lord,
And also something to digest;
Give me a healthy body, Lord,
With sense to keep it at its best.
Give me a healthy mind, good Lord,
To keep the good and pure in sight,
Which seeing sin is not appalled
But finds a way to set it right;
Give me a mind that is not bored,
That does not whimper, whine or sigh;
Don't let me worry overmuch
About the fussy thing called I.
Give me a sense of humor, Lord,
Give me the grace to see a joke,
To get some happiness from life
And pass it on to other folk.

Found in Chester Cathedral, England

IN old age,
Wandering on paths of beauty,
Lively may I walk.

Night chant of Navaho Indians
Southwestern United States

W E BESEECH THEE, O LORD, to hear our supplication on behalf of the dumb creation, who, after their kind, bless, praise, and magnify Thee forever. Grant that all cruelty may cease out of our land; and deepen our thankfulness to Thee for the faithful companionship of those whom we delight to call our friends.

Royal Society Prevention Cruelty to Animals Centenary Prayer (London 1924), England

O LORD JESUS CHRIST, Thou Good Shepherd of the sheep, who camest to seek the lost and to gather them into Thy fold, have compassion upon those who have wandered from Thee; feed those who hunger, cause the weary to lie down in Thy pastures, bind up those who are broken in heart, and strengthen those who are weak, that we, relying on Thy care and being comforted by Thy love, may abide in Thy guidance to our lives' end.

Ancient Collect Sixth Century

FOR THOSE ALSO, O LORD, THE humble beasts, who with us bear the burden and heat of the day, and offer their guileless lives for the well-being of their countries, we supplicate Thy great tenderness of heart, for Thou hast promised to save both man and beast, and great is Thy loving kindness, O Master, Saviour of the world.

Russian Liturgy
Tenth Century

GOD WHO HOLDS the children dear,
Care for me and keep me near.
What my worth and what my fortune,
All rests gently in God's hands.

Fortune comes and fortune goes,
But he who loves God fortune has.

Swedish Prayer

AKE US, O LORD, TO FLOURISH like pure lilies in the courts of Thine house, and to show forth to the faithful the fragrance of good works, and the example of a godly life, through Thy mercy and grace.

Mozarabic Liturgy, Spain
Sixth Century

Bless, O Lord, this house and all who dwell in it, as Thou wast pleased to bless the house of Abraham, Isaac, and Jacob; that within these walls may dwell an angel of light, and that we who dwell together in it may receive the abundant dew of heavenly blessing, and through Thy tenderness rejoice in peace and quiet.

Gelasian Sacramentary
Sixth Century

As the fire under the stone floor of my dwelling place burns brightly to warm my house, so may the love of God warm my heart and the hearts of those who step over my threshold.

Formosan Prayer

H KING of Stars!
Whether my house be dark or bright,
Never shall it be closed against any one,
Lest Christ close His house against me.

If there be a guest in your house
And you conceal aught from him,
'Tis not the guest that will be without it,
But Jesus, Mary's son.

Anonymous, Ireland
Thirteenth Century
Translated by Kuno Meyer

ALMIGHTY and everlasting God, be Thou present with us in all our duties, and grant the protection of Thy presence to all that dwell in this house, that Thou mayest be known to be the Defender of this household and the Inhabitant of this dwelling.

Gelasian Sacramentary
Sixth Century

PEACE BE TO this house, and to all who dwell in it. Peace to them that enter, and to them that depart.

York Psalter
Sixteenth Century

35

 LORD, WE BESEECH THEE TO bless and prosper this Thy household; grant us sweet reasonableness in all our dealings with one another; make us large-hearted in helping and generous in criticizing; keep us from unkind words and from unkind silences. Make us quick to understand the needs and feelings of others; and grant that living in the brightness of Thy presence we may bring sunshine into cloudy places.

Lucy H. M. Soulsby, England
Twentieth Century

O GOD, THOU ART with me and it is Thy will that these outward tasks are given me to do; therefore I ask Thee, assist me, and through it all let me continue in Thy presence. Be with me in this my endeavor, accept the labor of my hands, fill my heart as always.

Brother Lawrence, France
Seventeenth Century

GREAT SPIRIT, help me never to judge another until I have walked in his moccasins for two weeks.

Sioux Indian Prayer
Western United States

EAVENLY FATHER, IN WHOM we live and move and have our being, we humbly pray Thee so to guide and govern us by Thy holy Spirit that in all the cares and occupations of our daily life we may never forget Thee, but remember that we are ever walking in Thy sight.

Ancient Collect
Fifth Century

GIVE UNTO US, O GOD, the girdle, the helmet, the breastplate, the sandals, the sword, — above all things, prayer. Grant us the power and opportunity of well-doing, that before the day of our departure may come, we may have wrought at least somewhat, whose good fruit may remain; that we may behold Thy presence in righteousness, and be satisfied with Thy glory.

Lancelot Andrewes, England
Seventeenth Century

FOUNTAIN OF LOVE, LOVE Thou our friends and teach them to love Thee with all their hearts, that they may think and speak and do only such things as are well-pleasing to Thee.

St. Anselm, France
Eleventh Century

O GOD, who enlightenest every man that cometh into the world, enlighten our hearts by the splendor of Thy grace, that we may be able to think, and to love, things worthy of Thy majesty.

Gregorian Sacramentary
Eighth Century

O GOD, who art the Light of the minds that know Thee,
The Life of the souls that seek Thee,
And the Strength of the thoughts that seek Thee,
Help us to know Thee that we may truly love Thee,
So to love Thee that we may fully serve Thee,
    Whose service is perfect freedom.

Gelasian Sacramentary
Sixth Century

ive us, Lord, a bit o' sun,
A bit o' work and a bit o' fun;
Give us all in the struggle and sputter
Our daily bread and a bit o' butter;
Give us health, our keep to make,
An' a bit to spare for others' sake;
Give us sense, for we're some of us duffers,
An' a heart to feel for all that suffers;
Give us, too, a bit of a song
And a tale, and a book to help us along.
An' give us our share o' sorrow's lesson
That we may prove how grief's a blessin'.
Give us, Lord, a chance to be
Our goodly best, brave, wise, and free,
Our goodly best for ourself, and others,
Till all men learn to live as brothers.

On the wall of an old inn
Lancaster, England

LORD, MAKE US worthy of all we ask to receive.

Source Unknown

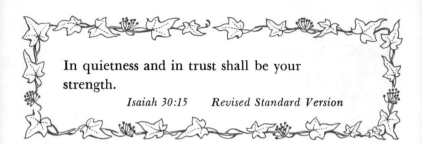

In quietness and in trust shall be your
strength.

Isaiah 30:15   Revised Standard Version

OH, MAKE my heart so still, so still,
When I am deep in prayer,
That I might hear the white-mist-wreaths
Losing themselves in air.

Japanese Prayer

O GOD OF PEACE who hast taught us that in return-
ing and rest we shall be saved, in quietness and in
confidence shall be our strength, by the might of Thy
Spirit lift us we pray Thee to Thy presence where
we may be still and know that Thou art God.

Book of Common Prayer
Sixteenth Century

GIVE UNTO US, O LORD, that quietness of mind in
which we can hear Thee speaking to us.

Anonymous, United States
Twentieth Century

SPEAK, LORD, FOR THY SERVANT
heareth.

Grant us ears to hear, eyes to see, wills to
obey, hearts to love; then declare what
Thou wilt, reveal what Thou wilt, command what Thou wilt, demand what Thou wilt.

Christina Rossetti, England
Nineteenth Century

GRANT CALMNESS and control of thought to those
who are facing uncertainty and anxiety: let their
heart stand fast, believing in the Lord. Be Thou all
things to all men, knowing each one and his petition,
each house and its need.

Russian Liturgy
Tenth Century

HERE needy he stands,
And I am he.

Osage Indian Prayer
Midwestern United States

41

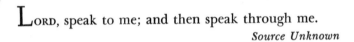

RANT US GRACE TO REST FROM all sinful deeds and thoughts, to surrender ourselves wholly unto Thee, and to keep our souls still before Thee like a still lake; that so the beams of Thy grace may be mirrored therein, and may kindle in our hearts the glow of faith, and love, and prayer.

May we, through such stillness and hope, find strength and gladness in Thee, O God, now and forevermore.

Joachim Embden
Sixteenth Century

O LORD, whose way is perfect, help us, we pray Thee, always to trust in Thy goodness; that, walking with Thee and following Thee in all simplicity, we may possess quiet and contented minds, and may cast all care on Thee, for Thou carest for us.

Christina Rossetti, England
Nineteenth Century

LORD, speak to me; and then speak through me.

Source Unknown

42

 HESE TEARS that dim my eyes,
This pain that plows my heart:
Take them, Lord, I give them Thee
As I give my gaiety.
Only let me keep as mine
The blessing that is here:
So to others I may be
Always warm with sympathy.

Anonymous, United States
Twentieth Century

How SILENTLY, how silently,
The wondrous gift is given;
So God imparts to human hearts
The blessings of His heaven.
No ear may hear His coming;
But in this world of sin
Where meek souls will receive Him still
The dear Christ enters in.

Phillips Brooks, United States
Nineteenth Century

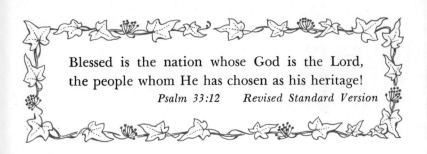

Blessed is the nation whose God is the Lord,
the people whom He has chosen as his heritage!

Psalm 33:12   Revised Standard Version

 RANDFATHER, GREAT SPIRIT, You have been always, and before You nothing has been. There is no one to pray to but You. The star nations all over the heavens are Yours, and Yours are the grasses of the earth. You are older than all need, older than all pain and prayer.

Grandfather, Great Spirit, all over the world the faces of living ones are alike. With tenderness they have come up out of the ground. Look upon our children, with children in their arms, that they may face the winds and walk the good road to the day of quiet.

Grandfather, Great Spirit, fill us with the light. Give us the strength to understand and the eyes to see. Teach us to walk the soft earth as relatives to all that live.

Help us, for without You we are nothing.

Sioux Indian Prayer
Western United States

GOD, WHO HAST MADE OF ONE blood all nations of men for to dwell on the face of the whole earth, and didst send Thy blessed Son to preach peace to them that are far off and to them that are nigh; grant that all men everywhere may seek after Thee and find Thee. Bring the nations into Thy fold, pour out Thy spirit upon all flesh and hasten Thy Kingdom.

Book of Common Prayer
Sixteenth Century

LORD, WHEN I look upon mine own life it seems Thou hast led me so carefully, so tenderly, Thou canst have attended to no one else; but when I see how wonderfully Thou hast led the world and art leading it, I am amazed that Thou hast time to attend to such as I.

St. Augustine, Africa
Fifth Century

GRANT THAT no word may fall from me, against my will, unfit for the present need.

Pericles, Greece
Fifth Century B.C.

THEY THAT ARE SNARED AND entangled in the utter lack of things needful for the body cannot set their minds upon Thee as they ought to do; but when they are deprived of the things which they so greatly desire, their hearts are cast down and quail for grief.

Have pity upon them, therefore, most merciful Father, and relieve their misery through Thy incredible riches, that, removing their urgent necessity, they may rise up to Thee in mind.

Thou, O Lord, providest enough for all men with Thy most bountiful hand. Give meat to the hungry and drink to the thirsty; comfort the sorrowful, cheer the dismayed and strengthen the weak; deliver the oppressed and give hope and courage to them that are out of heart.

Have mercy, O Lord, upon all forestallers, and upon all them that seek undue profits or unlawful gains. Turn Thou the hearts of them that live by cunning rather than by labor. Teach us that we stand daily and wholly in need of one another. And give us grace by hand and mind to add our proper share to the common stock; through Jesus Christ our Lord.

Queen Elizabeth I's Prayer Book
Sixteenth Century

 GOD, the Father,
Origin of Divinity,
Good beyond all that is good,
Fair beyond all that is fair,
In whom is calmness, peace, concord:

Do Thou make up the dissensions
Which divide us from each other.
And bring us back into the unity of love
Which to Thy divine nature
May bear some likeness.

As Thou art above all things,
Make us one by the unanimity
Of a good mind,
That through the embrace of charity,
And the bonds of godly affection
We spiritually may be one,
As well in ourselves
As in each other,
By that peace of Thine
Which makes all things peaceful.

Dionysius, Greece
Third Century

LOVING FATHER, WE BESEECH Thee most humbly, even with all our hearts, to pour out upon our enemies with bountiful hands whatsoever things Thou knowest may do them good: and chiefly a sound and uncorrupt mind, wherethrough they may know Thee and seek Thee in true charity, with their whole heart, and love us, Thy children, for Thy sake.

Let not their first hating of us turn to their harm, neither let us in any wise hurt them, seeing that we cannot do them good for want of ability.

Lord, we desire their amendment, and not their punishment. Separate them not from us by punishing them, but join and knit them to us by Thy favorable dealing with them.

And seeing we be all ordained to be citizens of the one everlasting city, let us begin to enter into that way here already by mutual love, which may bring us right forth hither.

English Prayer
Sixteenth Century

ALMIGHTY, EVERLASTING GOD, defend us from fear of the enemy, that, all danger being removed, we may serve Thee with untroubled minds.

Leonine Sacramentary
Seventh Century

THOU, O LORD, PROVIDETH enough for all men with Thy most liberal and bounteous hand, but whereas Thy gifts are, in respect to Thy goodness and free favor, made common to all men, we, through our naughtiness, niggardships and distrust, do make them private and peculiar. Correct Thou the thing which our iniquity hath put out of order, and let Thy goodness supply that which our niggardliness hath plucked away.

Queen Elizabeth I's Prayer Book
Sixteenth Century

O LORD GOD, when Thou givest to Thy servants to endeavor any great matter, grant us also to know that it is not the beginning, but the continuing of the same, until it be thoroughly finished, which yieldeth the true glory.

Sir Francis Drake, England
Sixteenth Century

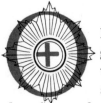 GOD, ALMIGHTY FATHER, King of kings and Lord of all rulers, grant that the hearts and minds of all who go out as leaders before us, the statesmen, the judges, the men of learning, and the men of wealth, may be so filled with the love of Thy laws, and of that which is righteous and life-giving, that they may serve as a wholesome salt unto the earth, and be worthy stewards of Thy good and perfect gifts.

From the Service of the Knights
of the Order of the Garter, England
Fourteenth Century

FROM THE MURMUR and subtlety of suspicion with which we vex one another, give us rest.

Make a new beginning and mingle again the kindred of the nations in the alchemy of love,

And with some fine essence of forbearance temper our minds.

Aristophanes, Greece
Fifth Century B.C.

GRANT UNTO OUR MINDS, O Lord, that they may rise up to Thee through the hardships of this world, and from these troubles come to Thee, and that with the eyes of our minds opened we may behold the noble fountain of all good things, even Thee.

Grant us health for our minds' eyes, that we may fasten them upon Thee, and scatter the mist that now hangeth before our minds' sight, and let Thy light lighten our eyes; for Thou art the brightness of the true Light.

Thou art the comfortable resting-place of the righteous, and Thou enablest them to see Thee.

Thou art the Beginning and the End of all things.

Thou bearest up all things without effort.

Thou art the Way, and the Guide, and the Bourne whither the way leadeth;

And to Thee all men are hastening.

Boethius, Italy
Sixth Century

51

Blessing and glory and wisdom and thanksgiving and honor and power and might be to our God for ever and ever!

Rev. 7:12   Revised Standard Version

LORD OUR GOD, WITHOUT whose will and pleasure not a sparrow can fall to the ground, grant us in times of trouble to be patient without murmuring or despair, and in prosperity to acknowledge Thy gifts, and to confess that all our endowments come from Thee, O Father of lights, who givest liberally and upbraidest not. Give us, by Thy holy spirit, a willing heart and a ready hand to use all Thy gifts to Thy praise and glory.

Thomas Cranmer, England
Sixteenth Century

IN THIS HOUR of this day, fill us, O Lord, with Thy mercy, that rejoicing throughout the whole day, we may take delight in Thy praise.

Sarum Breviary, England
Eleventh Century

OME, LET US PRAISE GOD, FOR He is exceeding great; let us bless God, for He is very good.

He made all things; the sun to rule by day, the moon to shine by night.

He made the great whale, and the elephant; and the little worm that crawleth upon the ground.

The little birds sing praises to God when they warble sweetly in the green shade.

The brooks and rivers praise God when they murmur melodiously among the smooth pebbles.

I will praise God with my voice; for I may praise Him, though I am but a little child.

A few years ago, and I was a little infant, and my tongue was dumb within my mouth:

And I did not know the great name of God, for my reason was not come unto me.

But now I can speak, and my tongue shall praise Him; I can think of all His kindness, and my heart shall love Him.

Let Him call me, and I will come unto Him; let Him command, and I will obey Him.

When I am older, I will praise Him better; and I will never forget God, so long as my life remaineth in me.

Anna Letitia Barbauld, England
Early Nineteenth Century

LET ALL the Lord's bairns praise Him,
And let us appropriate the truth of
His faith.
We live in the Lord by His grace;
And life we receive in His Messiah.
For a great day has shined upon us;
And marvelous is He who hath given us
His glory.
Let us, therefore, all of us unite together
In the name of the Lord:
And let us honor Him in His goodness:
And let our faces shine in His light;
And let our hearts meditate in His love,
By night and by day,
Let us exult with the joy of the Lord.

The Oldest Christian Hymnbook
First Century

GREAT ART THOU, O Lord, and greatly to be
praised; great is Thy power, and Thy wisdom is in-
finite. Thee would we praise without ceasing. Thou
callest us to delight in Thy praise, for Thou hast
made us for Thyself, and our hearts find no rest
until we rest in Thee.

St. Augustine, Africa
Fifth Century

PLEASURE it is
To hear, I wis,
The birdes sing.
The deer in the dale,
The sheep in the vale,
The corn springing.
God's purveyance
For sustenance
It is for man.
Then we always
To Him give praise,
And thank Him then,
And thank Him then.

William Cornish, England
Sixteenth Century

THANK YOU for the world so sweet,
Thank You for the food we eat,
Thank You for the birds that sing,
Thank You, God, for everything.

Source Unknown

LMIGHTY GOD, WHO HAST blessed the earth that it should be fruitful and bring forth everything necessary for the life of man, and hast commanded us to work with quietness and eat our own bread; bless us in all our labors, and grant us such seasonable weather that we may gather in the fruits of the earth, and ever rejoice in Thy goodness, to the praise of Thy holy Name.

American Prayer Book
Eighteenth Century

THE EYES OF ALL things do look up and trust in Thee, O Lord. Thou givest them their meat in due season, Thou dost open Thine hand and fillest with blessing everything living. Good Lord, bless us and all Thy gifts, which we receive of Thy bounteous liberality.

Queen Elizabeth I's Prayer Book
Sixteenth Century

GIVE US grateful hearts, our Father, for all Thy mercies, and make us mindful of the needs of others.

Book of Common Prayer
Sixteenth Century

WHAT GOD gives, and what we take,
'Tis a gift for Christ, His sake:
Be the meal of beans and pease,
God be thanked for those and these:
Have we flesh or have we fish,
All are fragments from His dish.

Robert Herrick, England
Seventeenth Century

O THOU, who kindly dost provide
For every creature's want!
We bless Thee, God of nature wide,
For all Thy goodness lent:
And, if it please Thee, heavenly Guide,
May never worse be sent;
But, whether granted or denied,
Lord, bless us with content!

Robert Burns, Scotland
Eighteenth Century

57

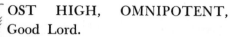

OST HIGH, OMNIPOTENT, Good Lord.

Thine be the praise, the glory, the honor, and all benediction.

Be Thou praised, my Lord, with all Thy creatures, above all Brother Sun, who gives the day and lightens us therewith.

And he is beautiful and radiant with great splendor, of Thee, Most High, he bears similitude.

Be Thou praised, my Lord, of Sister Moon and the stars, in the heaven hast Thou formed them, clear and precious and comely.

Be Thou praised, my Lord, of Brother Wind, and of the air, and the cloud, and of fair and of all weather, by the which Thou givest to Thy creatures sustenance.

Be Thou praised, my Lord, of Sister Water, which is much useful and humble and precious and pure.

Be Thou praised, my Lord, of Brother Fire, by which Thou hast lightened the night, and he is beautiful and joyful and robust and strong.

Be Thou praised, my Lord, of our Sister Mother Earth, which sustains and hath us in rule, and produces divers fruits with colored flowers and herbs.

Be Thou praised, my Lord, of those who pardon for Thy love and endure sickness and tribulations.

Be Thou praised, my Lord, of our Sister Bodily Death, from whom no man living may escape.

Praise ye and bless my Lord, and give Him thanks, and serve Him with great humility.

St. Francis of Assisi, Italy
Thirteenth Century

THOU HAST GIVEN so much to me,
Give one thing more — a grateful heart;
Not thankful when it pleaseth me,
As if Thy blessings had spare days,
But such a heart whose pulse may be
Thy praise.

George Herbert, England
Seventeenth Century

GRANT ME, O LORD, THE royalty of inward happiness, and the serenity which comes from living close to Thee.

Daily renew in me the sense of joy, and let the Eternal Spirit of the Father dwell in my soul and body, filling every corner of my heart with light and grace, so that, bearing about with me the infection of a good courage, I may be a diffuser of life, and may meet all ills and cross accidents with gallant and high-hearted happiness, giving Thee thanks always for all things.

Lucy H. M. Soulsby, England
Twentieth Century

HERE a little child I stand
Heaving up my either hand;
Cold as paddocks though they be,
Here I lift them up to Thee,
For a benison to fall
On our meat and on us all.

Robert Herrick, England
Seventeenth Century

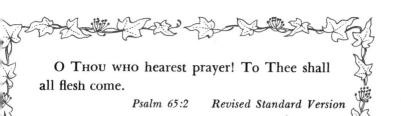

O Thou who hearest prayer! To Thee shall all flesh come.

Psalm 65:2   *Revised Standard Version*

Old Testament Prayers   *Revised Standard Version*

HE LORD WATCH BETWEEN YOU and me, when we are absent one from the other.

Genesis 31:49

The Lord bless you and keep you:

The Lord make His face to shine upon you, and be gracious to you:

The Lord lift up His countenance upon you, and give you peace.

Numbers 6:24–26

O Lord my God, I am but a little child; I do not know how to go out or come in. Give Thy servant therefore an understanding mind to govern Thy people, that I may discern between good and evil.

I Kings 3:7, 9

THINE, O LORD, IS THE GREAT-
ness, and the power, and the glory, and
the victory, and the majesty; for all that
is in the heavens and in the earth is
Thine; Thine is the kingdom, O Lord,
and Thou art exalted as head above all. Both riches
and honor come from Thee, and Thou rulest over
all. In Thy hand are power and might; and in Thy
hand it is to make great and to give strength to all.
And now we thank Thee, our God, and praise Thy
glorious name.

I Chron. 29:11–13

IN THEE, O LORD, do I take refuge; let me never
be put to shame!
Be Thou to me a rock of refuge, a strong fortress,
to save me, for Thou art my rock and my fortress.

Psalm 71:1, 3

LET THY WORK be manifest to Thy servants, and
Thy glorious power to their children.
Let the favor of the Lord our God be upon us, and
establish Thou the work of our hands upon us,
Yes, the work of our hands establish Thou it.

Psalm 90:16, 17

FATHER, I THANK THEE THAT Thou hast heard me. I knew that Thou hearest me always.

John 11:41, 42

Now is my soul troubled. And what shall I say, "Father, save me from this hour?" No, for this purpose I have come to this hour. Father, glorify Thy name.

John 12:27, 28

Holy Father, keep them in Thy name which Thou hast given me, that they may be one, even as we are one.

John 17:11

Father, if Thou art willing, remove this cup from me; nevertheless not my will, but Thine, be done.

Luke 22:42

Father, forgive them; for they know not what they do.

Luke 23:34

F ATHER, into Thy hands I commit my spirit!

Luke 23:46

 ur Father who art in heaven,
Hallowed be Thy name.
Thy kingdom come,
Thy will be done,
On earth as it is in heaven.
Give us this day our daily bread;
And forgive us our debts,
As we also have forgiven our debtors;
And lead us not into temptation,
But deliver us from evil.

Matthew 6:9–13